This is a book celebrating
all of the wonderful things
you share together.

♥

On the
day you were born,
everything changed
for the better.

WELCOME TO THE WORLD!

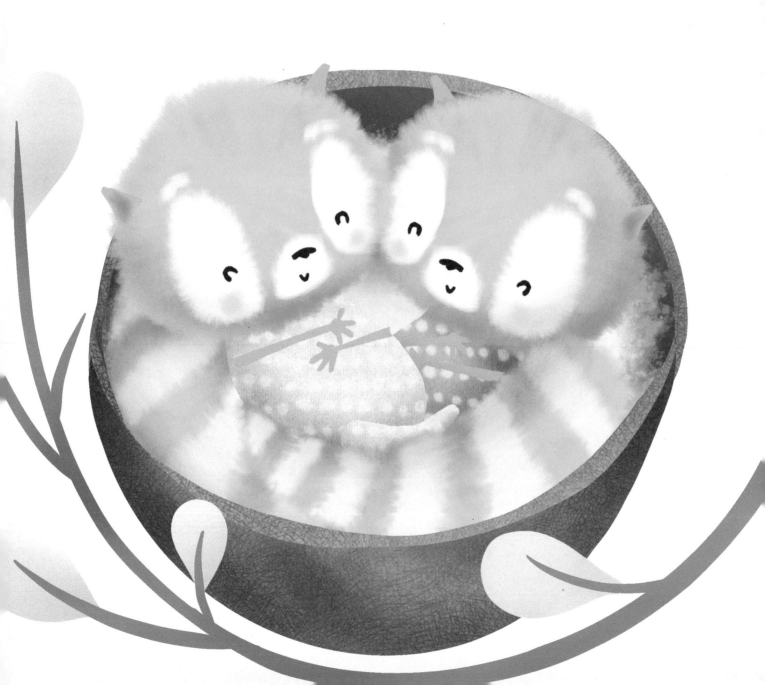

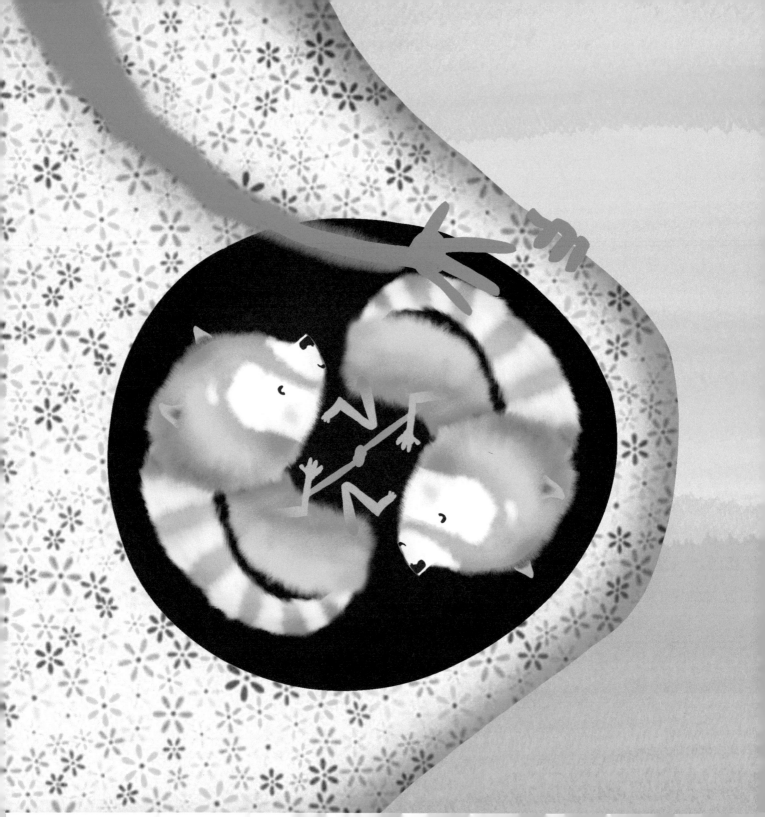

You are very lucky to be twins.

From your very first moment
you have had each other.

You are friends, companions...

...team mates for life!

You will always have someone to keep you company.

Someone to play with,

(and occasionally squabble with!).

You will get to discover
the world together.

Just think of the adventures
you will have!

You have so much to explore.

Together::

...side by side...

... with
someone who is
always <u>on</u> your side!

You have
so much
to share...

...Your first home.

Your birthday!

. . . and lasts.

Your jokes...

...and your secrets.

Your hopes
and dreams.

... and your fears.

..and so much love.

Miracles
really do...

...come
in
pairs.

'The Things We Share - Twins'

An original concept by Lucy Tapper & Steve Wilson
© Tapper Wilson Creative Ltd
Written by Lucy Tapper & Steve Wilson
Illustrated by Lucy Tapper
First edition 2021

FROMLUCY, STUDIO 3 PIXON COURT, PIXON LANE, TAVISTOCK, DEVON, UK, PL19 9AZ

Create your own amazing, unique book to be treasured forever.

www.fromlucy.com

Made in United States
Troutdale, OR
01/02/2024

16613657R00021